Roger Wagner's visual world is imm
juxtaposition of familiar and unfa
ancient and modern, a solitary woman threatened by men with stones
and men with cellphone cameras, so often within a landscape of overwhelming radiance, local and unearthly all at once. Here these images
are woven around with reflective prose and with poetry that has the
same unsettling radiance. A book of transfigurations.

Rowan Williams

Roger Wagner, in my mind, is one of the most important artists work-
ing today. *The Nearer You Stand* captures his immense gift as a painter,
and provides a glimpse into the realm of disciplined discourse that leads
to these indelible images. His 'discourse' happens to be his own poetry,
a peek into his adroit integrative power of communication that speaks
powerfully into our souls.

Makoto Fujimura, artist

These poems and pictures have given me great pleasure. They have
been woven together with much skill.

Anthony Thwaite, poet and critic

Although we rarely use 'truth' as a value of modern art, it is unavoid-
able in considering the poetry and painting of Roger Wagner. His
vision is particularly his, through its clear-eyed clarity and strength, yet
it is recognisable and resonant within a tradition of English painters
and poets. This lineage is deep-rooted and as vital now as it ever was,
but perhaps it is the note of quiet conviction that makes these poems,
paintings and prints so compelling and unusual today.

Christopher le Brun, President of the Royal Academy of Arts

Roger Wagner is an artist who calls our attention to a world infused with the divine. His poems follow suit: intelligent, neatly metric but often catching us off guard. His poetry, like his images, frames the density of the unignorable mystery and the call of the transcendent to restless hearts. This is a beautiful and spiritually rich book to spend proper time with.

Mark Oakley, author of The Splash of Words

Coleridge said that poetry should 'awaken the mind's attention' and remove the 'film of familiarity' we have thrown over the world, and the same could also be said of good visual art. By a deft combination of both art forms, Roger Wagner's new work does just what Coleridge asks. Here are paintings and poems that help us to see in a new way, and challenge our habits and assumptions. Modern scenes are re-imagined as alive with biblical resonance, and biblical scenes are brought into new relevance and focus. Coleridge also hoped poetry would reveal new 'loveliness and wonders', and in luminous, often numinous art, and in precise and plangent verse, Roger Wagner restores our sense of wonder even as he sharpens our vision.

Malcolm Guite, author and poet

Roger Wagner is an illuminator in the rich medieval sense of one who makes images and text sing together. I appreciated an imagination that breaks down barriers between East and West, past and present, darkness and light. Be prepared to be startled by his profound simplicity.

Esther de Waal, author

The Nearer You Stand

Poems and Images

Roger Wagner

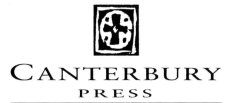

CANTERBURY
PRESS
Norwich

© Roger Wagner 2019

First published in 2019 by the Canterbury Press Norwich
Editorial office
3rd Floor, Invicta House
108–114 Golden Lane
London EC1Y 0TG, UK
www.canterburypress.co.uk

Canterbury Press is an imprint of Hymns Ancient & Modern Ltd
(a registered charity)

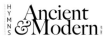

Hymns Ancient & Modern® is a registered trademark of
Hymns Ancient & Modern Ltd
13A Hellesdon Park Road, Norwich,
Norfolk NR6 5DR, UK

British Library Cataloguing in Publication data

A catalogue record for this book is available
from the British Library

978 1 78622 222 0

Typeset by Regent Typesetting Ltd
Printed and bound in Great Britain by
Ashford Colour Press Ltd

Contents

Introduction 1

Medusa's view of the world 4
Writing in the Dust *The men taken in hypocrisy* 8
Hougoumont Crucifix 12
Brightwell Barrow 16
I turn the pages of my life 22
I saw the Seraphim 26
The Mirrors 34
Abraham and the Angels I 38
Seven Songs for Isseos 44
 Deir al-Zor, Thursday 10 October 1996 44
 I 46
 Deir al-Zor, Wednesday 13 October 1999 48
 II 50
 New Haven, Wednesday 14 October 2009 52
 III *Ode 39 from The Odes of Solomon* 54
 New Haven, Wednesday 14 October 2009 56
 IV *From the Dura-Europos psalm-book* 58
 Oxford, April 2017 60
 V 63
 Aleppo, Thursday 14 October 1999 68
 VI *Ruth and Boaz* 71
 Oxford, Wednesday 5 April 2017 76
 VII 78
The Bright Day 82
Abraham and the Angels II 84

Saint Martin at Andethanna   87
Walking on Water   97
I turned the pages of my life   103
Rest on the Flight into Egypt   107
The Road to Emmaus   109

Acknowledgements   116

Ut pictura poesis: erit quae, si propius stes
te capiat magis, et quaedam, si longius abstes;

A poem is like a painting:
one strikes your fancy more the nearer you stand;
another the farther away.
Horace, *Ars Poetica* (lines 361–2)

Introduction

The genesis of this collection of poems and images was a small hand-bound notebook that I was given as a birthday present. The quality of the binding suggested that whatever filled it must rise to the occasion, but did the deckle-edged pages invite images or text? In the end they seemed to demand both.

In my twenties, I produced two books of poems and images, which I printed on a treadle press and bound by hand. When I showed these to the poet Peter Levi, he suggested that for me poetry and painting seemed to belong together, and counselled that I should always try to preserve that connection. Since then at decade intervals I have produced illustrated translations of successive books of the psalms, but have never again illustrated my own poetry, which (until the gift of the notebook) I had almost stopped writing.

There were several reasons for this, but one at least was that in western culture there has been no established practice of putting poetry and images alongside one another, even though theoretically they have been thought to belong together.

The quotation from Horace (that I use as an epigraph and title) which begins *ut pictura poesis*, 'as is painting so is poetry', has been used since the sixteenth century to argue that poetry and painting are sister arts. Long before Horace, the ancient Greek poet Simonides is reputed to have said that 'painting is mute poetry, poetry a speaking picture'. Greek painters and sculptors often seem to have taken their subjects from the poets, while Greek poets sometimes included in their work what was called *ekphrsasis* – describing in poetry a visual work of art – like Homer's description of the shield of Achilles.

This kind of mutual influence has been common throughout the course of western culture. Yet while there have certainly been great artists like Michelangelo who were also considerable poets, few have actually tried to combine the two arts. Examples like the Ruthwell cross (where a carved crucifix is inscribed with a poem in which the cross tells its own story) are as rare as hen's teeth. Those like William Blake who did try to make this combination found little encouragement. Blake discovered he could only do so by printing his books himself. The many now lost manuscripts and designs that he showed to publishers were all turned down. 'Well', he would say, 'it is published elsewhere' (meaning in heaven) 'and beautifully bound'.

Chinese culture has a very different tradition. Wang Wei, one of the great eighth-century classical poets, was also reputed to be a founding figure of Chinese landscape painting. Although the images of his *Wang River* sequence have not survived, the combination of poetry and imagery that they represented became over the centuries something like a standard procedure. There were two aspects to this combination. On the one hand the art of calligraphy provided a kind of middle term between painting and poetry, while on the other the practice of meditation provided a motivation and focus that both arts could serve.

Within Christianity it has, in a similar way, been in the context of worship that texts and images have most naturally come together; at first in church buildings and then from the sixth century onwards in illuminated manuscripts. These started with 'chrysography' – writing initial letters or whole words in gold – and rapidly progressed to including images in the margins and interstices of the text. In a medieval scriptorium the person who added the gold and the images was known as an *illuminator* – one who cast light.

In the Bible, the light of God is that which shines in the darkness of the human soul, opening our eyes, bringing spiritual sight and revealing the truth. The corollary is that the darkness of evil is real, as is the possibility of spiritual blindness. In Horace's *Ars Poetica*, finding the way into a poem or picture may be a matter of establishing the right viewing distance ('the nearer you stand … the farther away'). Where spiritual issues are concerned, a similar principle may be involved but here the stakes are raised.

The two poems that bookend this collection both dwell on such high-stake questions. What might the world look like to the snake-haired gorgon of Greek mythology whose gaze turned all to stone? How did the world change when the two disciples at Emmaus found that 'their eyes were opened'? In different ways themes of this kind run through the whole sequence.

The poems and images in the first half of the book often revolve around different ways of seeing and being seen. The central sequence of seven poems was inspired by the oldest known Christian building: a site where images and words were placed alongside one another, as an early Christian congregation (like those Chinese scroll collectors who would write their own poetic responses on to ancient paintings) literally wrote themselves into their pictures. Following from this, the pictures and poems towards the end of the collection dwell more on how vision is shaped by action: what we see by what we do.

Shaped but not determined. There is often something surprising about a moment of vision: a moment of seeing things as they truly are. It can arrive like a kind of unexpected grace, which is gone almost as soon as it has come, and leaves us to make of it what we can. It is a characteristic that has been noted of even the most overwhelming revelations, and is evident in the three phrases that outline the climactic moment of the supper at Emmaus:

Their eyes were opened and they recognised him,
and he disappeared from their sight.
Luke 24.31

Medusa's view of the world
What the Gorgon saw

I see a world of stone,
Of statues without breath,
Beyond the writhing of my skull
A world as still as death.

I stumble through a door,
And for a moment see
A world of breathing beauty where
The statues are set free.

They leap and whirl around
Their blue shifts swirl about
Their hair is flame, is flowing gold
They sing, they dance, they shout.

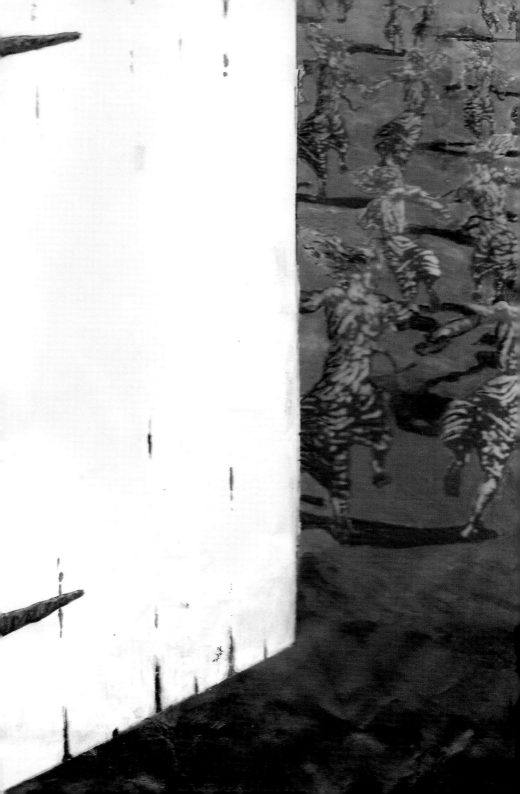

And then a world of stone:
Of statues without breath,
Beyond the writhing of my skull
A world as still as death.

It was complete illusion.
There is only what I see.
This solid world, this world of stone
Defines reality.

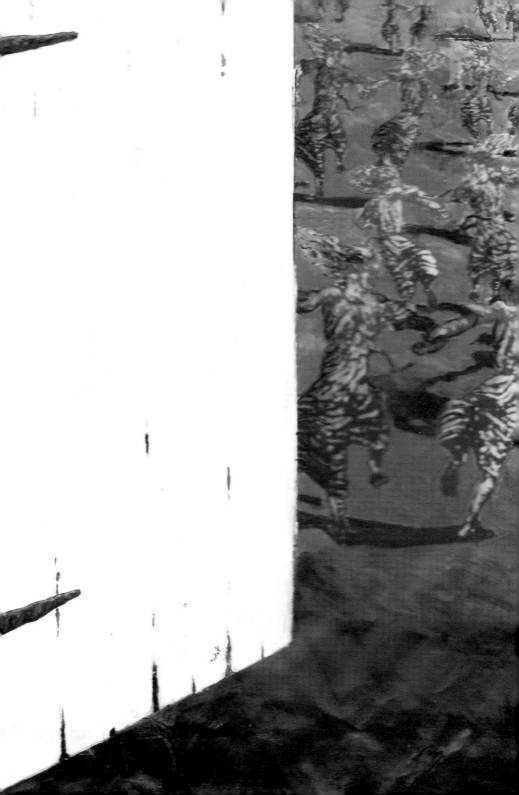

Writing in the Dust
The men taken in hypocrisy

*'The scribes and the Pharisees brought unto him a woman taken
in adultery; and when they had set her in the midst, they say unto
him, "Master, this woman was taken in adultery, in the very act."
Now Moses in the law commanded us, that such should be stoned:
but what sayest thou? ... But Jesus stooped down, and with his
finger wrote on the ground'*
John 8.3–6 (AV)

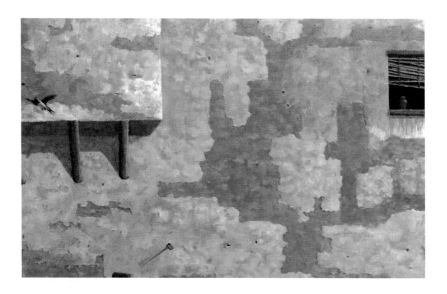

The beating of a swallow's wings,
A stone jar poised as if to fall,
A fierce and unforgiving sun
That beats upon a whitewashed wall

That finds and tracks each human flaw
And reads the writing in the dust
Of broken hopes and powdered dreams
And love reclassified as lust.

Where images of shameful death
Describe a life defined by blame,
The beatings of a swallow's wings
Above a place of public shame

Are like the barest breath of grace
That stirs the unforgiving air:
That shifts the gaze and leads the eye
Beyond the camera's fatal stare

To where one writes in grit and dust
– Of dry bones in a bone-dry place,
Of broken hopes and powdered dreams –
The unseen, unhoped, words of grace

Which free accuser and accused
And spell out where that way begins:
A motion like a breath of grace
The beating of a swallow's wings.

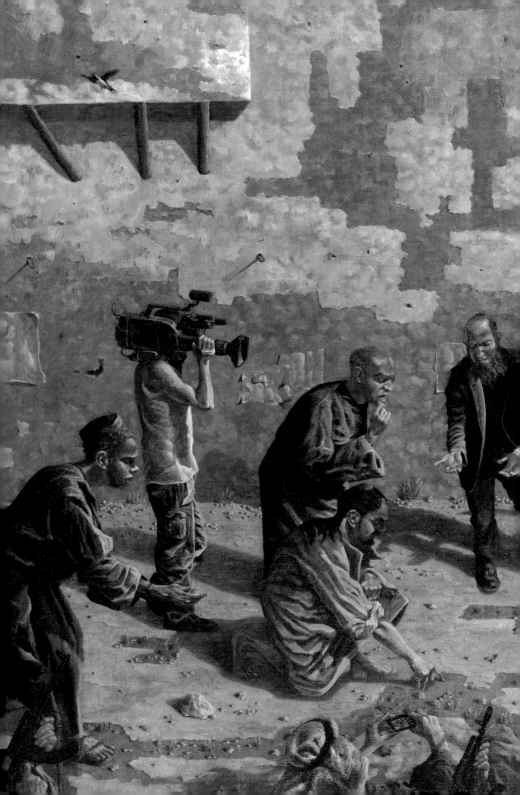

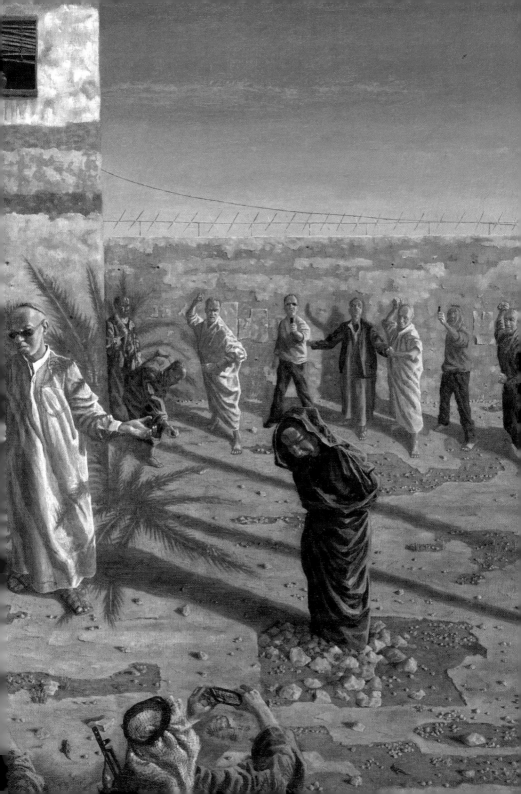

Hougoumont Crucifix

Les murs sont couverts d'inscriptions. Il y a des noms français avec des points d'exclamation, signes de colère. On a reblanchi le mur en 1849. Les nations s'y insultaient.
Victor Hugo, Les Misérables

When Victor Hugo found the farm
In which the cross of Christ had burned
He saw graffitied on a wall
Thick screeds of names could be discerned

Where scratched and inked around the cross
By tourists, pilgrims, grieving wives
Were signatures that signified
A wastage of six thousand lives:

A morning and an afternoon
The place where a great battle turned,
A chapel near to Waterloo
In which the peace of Europe burned.

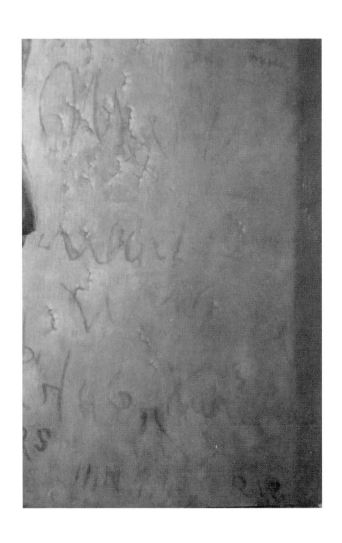

Beneath that whitewash Hugo claimed
Were older layers of scribbled names
Where echoes from the warring dead
Fought out in words their rival claims

Like some unvalued, ancient harm,
Both unappeased and under-priced
That burned the gates and burned the farm
And burnt the legs and feet of Christ.

But burnt out on the cross of Christ
Touched by a harm that all harm mends
A peace where none is under-priced
A place where every battle ends.

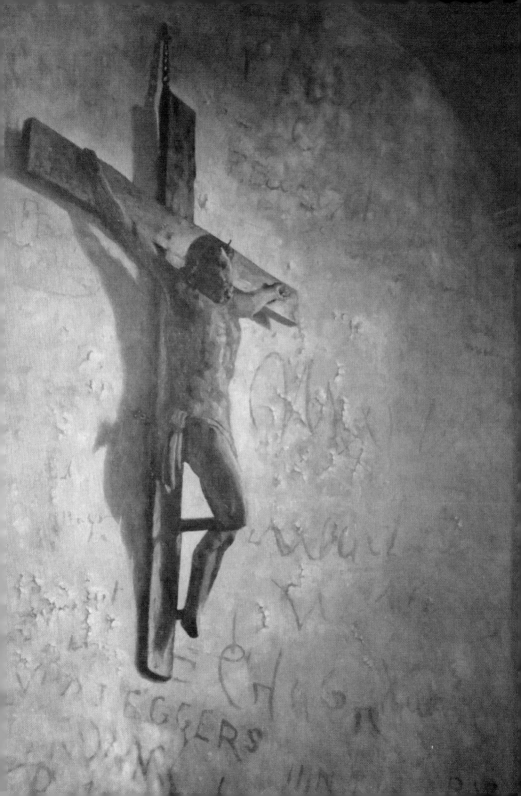

Brightwell Barrow

Three stations of that afternoon
Recur in sky-filled dreams at night:
The first a mountain range of cloud
So high I could not guess its height

Beneath which Brightwell Barrow stood
As though a foothill of that sky:
A base camp for the mind's ascent
Beyond where any bird could fly.

The second was a distant man
Who swept a field for hidden gold,
For which the whole field might be bought
Though all that he possessed were sold.

The third a smoke of small black birds
That rose and passed far overhead;
A glitter of white birds that rose
And laced that blackness like bright thread.

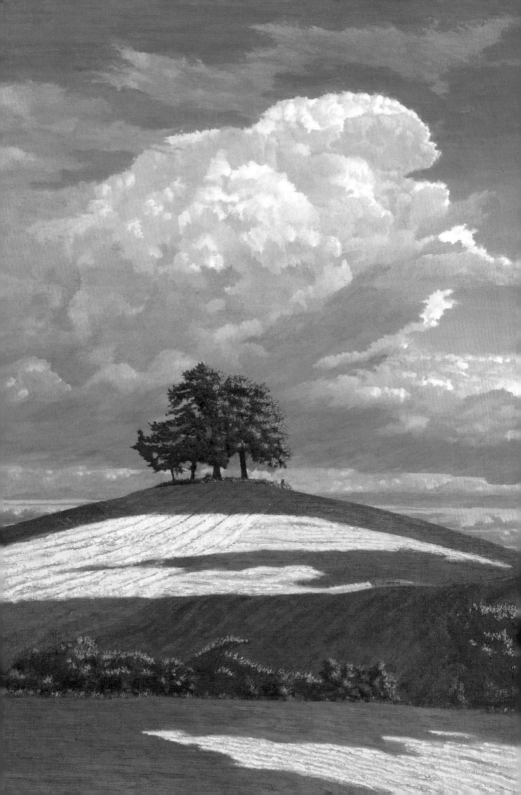

Returning as the sun fell down
I saw the man still seeking gold,
For which the whole field might be bought
Though all that he possessed were sold.

But now the mountain range of cloud
Was suds and sweepings of that sky.
Great ages of geology
While I was walking had flowed by.

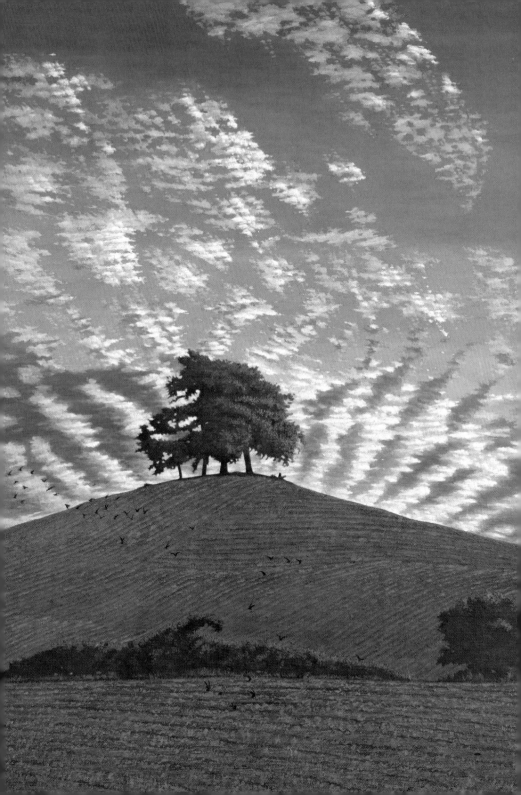

There is here no abiding gold,
Our dreams are flowing through a glass
And beauty is each moment's gift:
We kiss our hand and watch it pass.

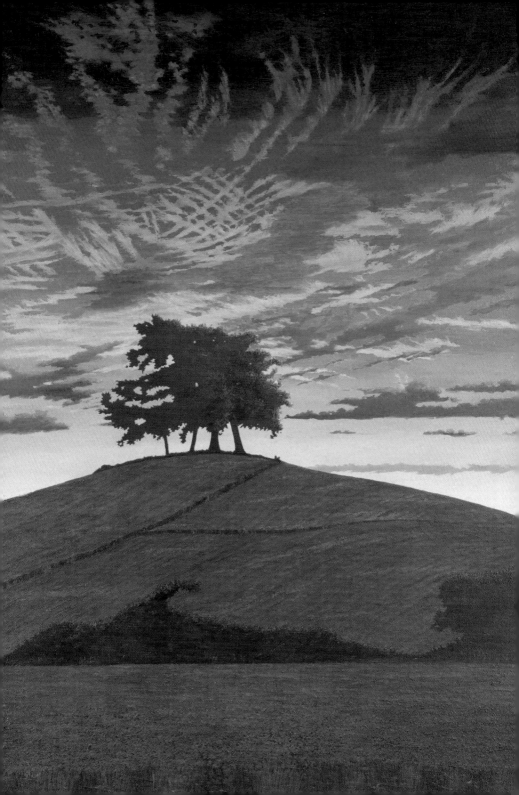

I turn the pages of my life

I turn the pages of my life
And watch its parables unroll:
The Saltings where a winter tree
First spoke into my waking soul

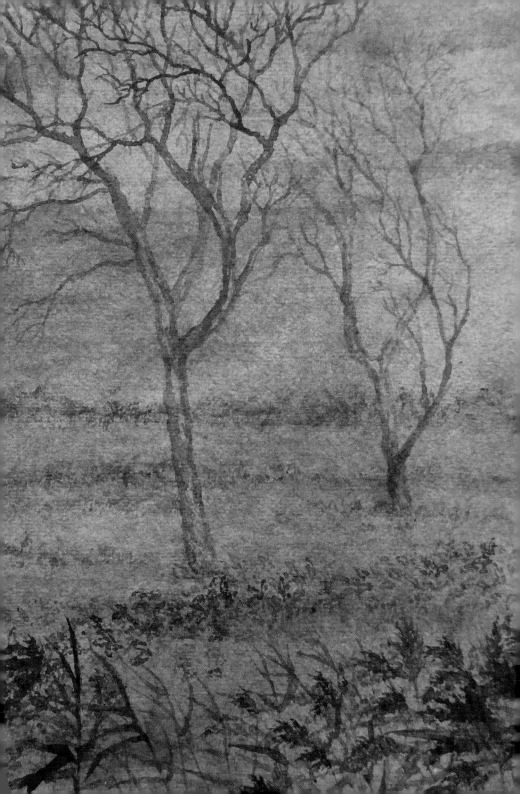

I turn the pages of my life
And see a tree full-leafed, entire
A glory burning in a field
A blaze that salts my soul with fire.

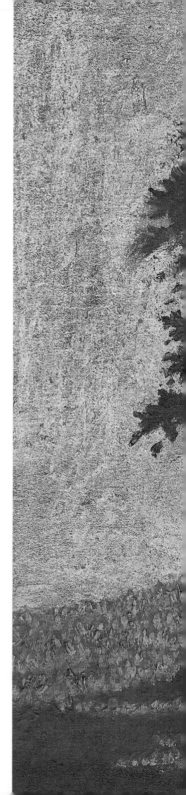

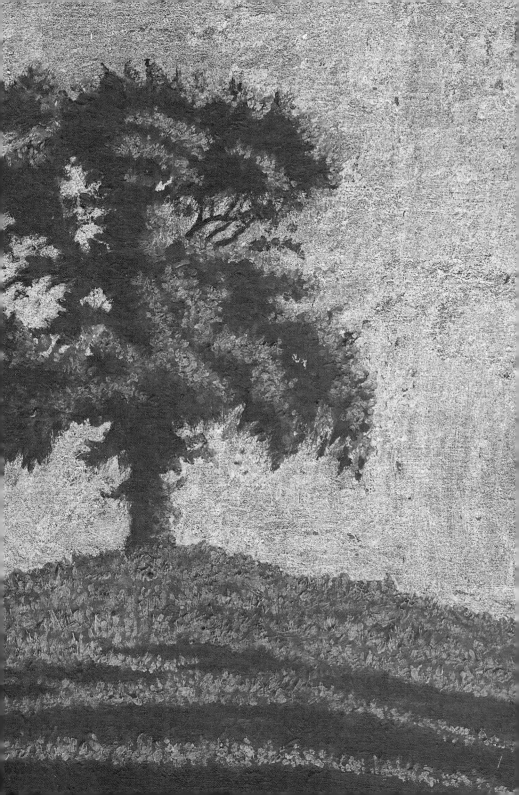

I saw the Seraphim

*The harvest is the end of the world
and the reapers are angels*
Matthew 13.39 (AV)

I saw the Seraphim one summer's night
Reaping it seemed a field of endless wheat.
I heard their voices through the fading light
Wild, strange and yet intolerably sweet.
The hour such beauty first was born on earth
A dawn of sifting had that day begun
For some would not endure love's second birth
Preferring their own darkness to that sun.
And still love's sun must rise upon our night
For nothing can be hidden from its heat
And in that summer evening's fading light
I saw his angels gather in the wheat.
Like beaten gold their beauty smote the air
And tongues of flame were streaming in their hair.

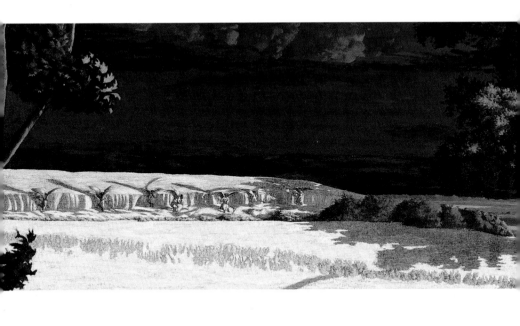

And tongues of flame were streaming in their hair
And flames of fire were dancing in the heat
And through the liquid dancing of that air
I saw the seraphim bring in the wheat.
Yet some have entertained them unaware
And with unearthly guests sat down to eat
And found that meal became itself a prayer
A trysting place where earth and heaven meet.
As in a dream once Jacob saw a stair
With fire-bright angels moving up and down
And dreaming saw the gate of heaven where
An endless love stood as that stairway's crown:
That moves the stars with passionate desire
And makes his angels flames of burning fire.

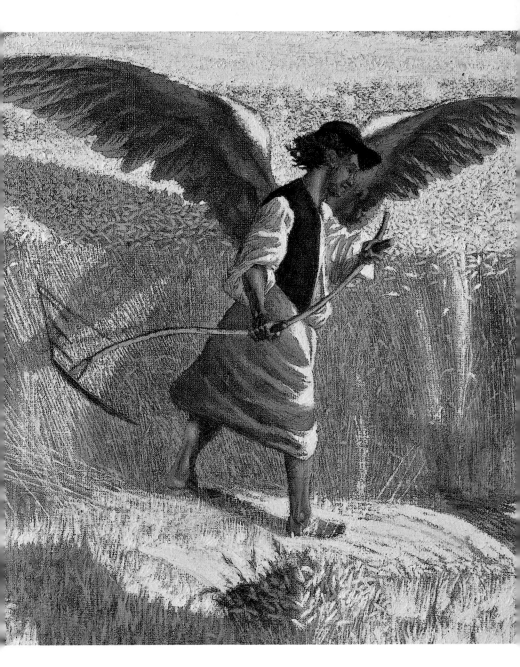

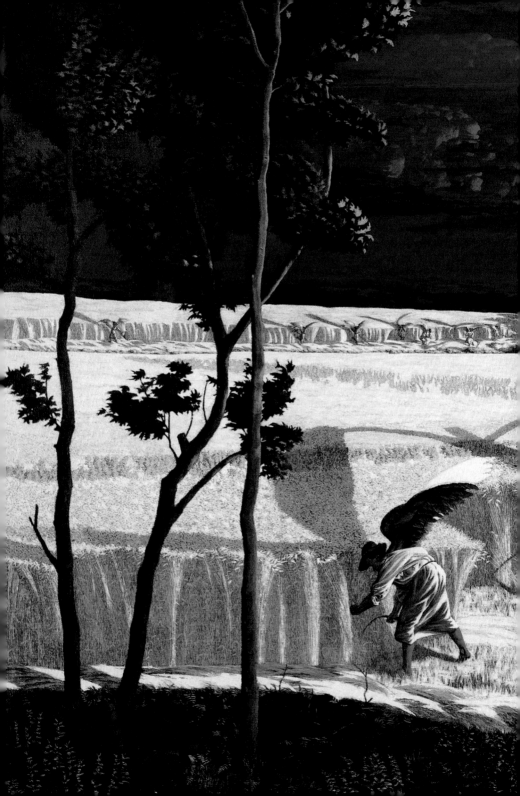

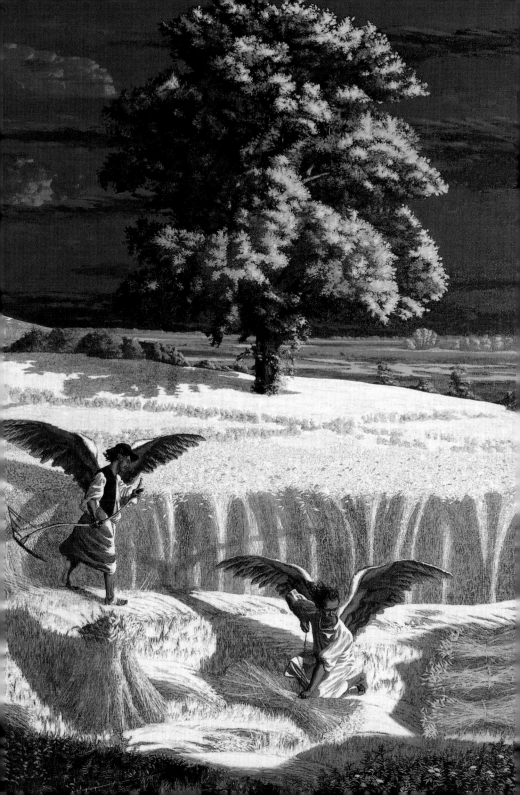

He makes winds his angels
His servants flames of fire
Psalm 104.4

Who hears the ocean roaring in a tree
That rustles like a thousand angels' wings
And feels the rising wind he cannot see
Is seeing to the burning heart of things.
For as a book has pages stamped with ink
While yet some meaning rustles all its leaves
So all things are as words that forge a link
Between the writer and the one who reads.
And that unnamed I AM that forged all things
Whose presence is the ocean in a tree
That rustles like a thousand angels' wings
Stirred by a wind no human eye can see
Breathes hope into the ash where hopes expire
In winds that flame with Pentecostal fire.

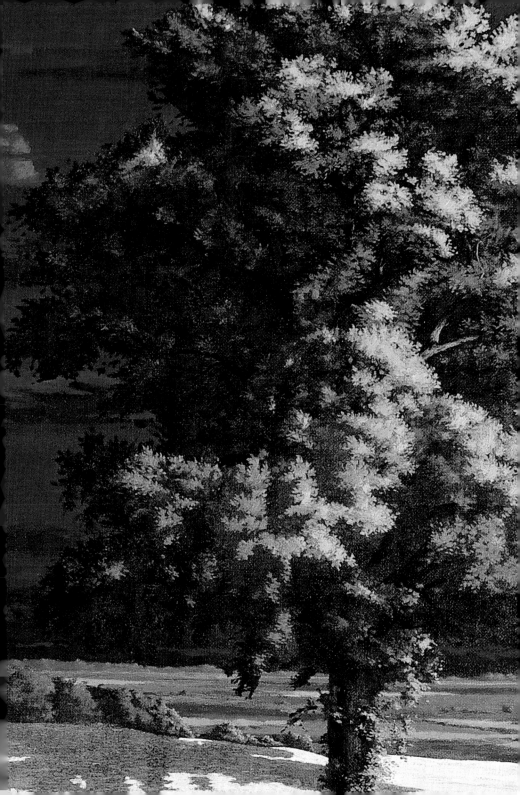

The Mirrors

So God created man in his own image,
in the image of God he created him;
male and female created he them.
Genesis 1.27 (AV)

At his gate was laid a beggar named Lazarus
Luke 16.20

Then he turned towards the woman
and said to Simon,
'Do you see this woman?'
Luke 7.44

The mirrors of Almighty God
Have blankets made of plastic bags
Beneath the bridge at Charing Cross
Near where the river's current drags

Its burden of black stinking mud
And rubber tyres and broken oars
They lie like Lazarus at night
When rich men's guard dogs licked his sores.

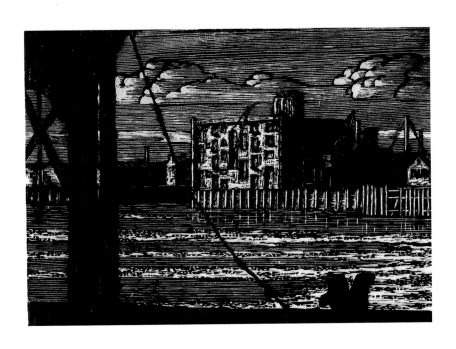

The mirrors of Almighty God
Have Oxford street as their love bower
They leave their names in public phones
And sell themselves for half an hour

Or find their work in adult shows
That line the streets off Soho square
Performing like King Herod's niece
For those who buy their right to stare.

The mirrors of Almighty God
More deeply than all skill could mend
In love's first garden looked on death
And looking cracked from end to end.

But if a face could crack a glass
The reflex of that would be true
That in the beauty of a face
A broken mirror is made new.

So one who came from Simon's house
Found that her face was wet with tears
But shining just as Moses did
When love had washed away his fears.

And once among the Gadarenes
The naked man they came to find
Sat looking into God's own face
Clothed, healed and in his right mind.

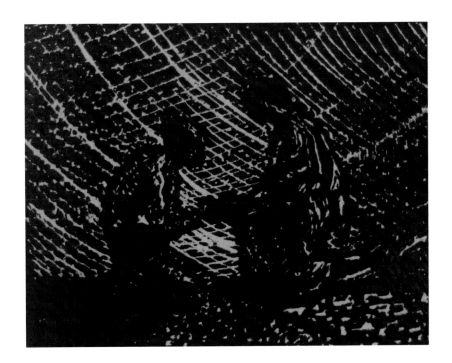

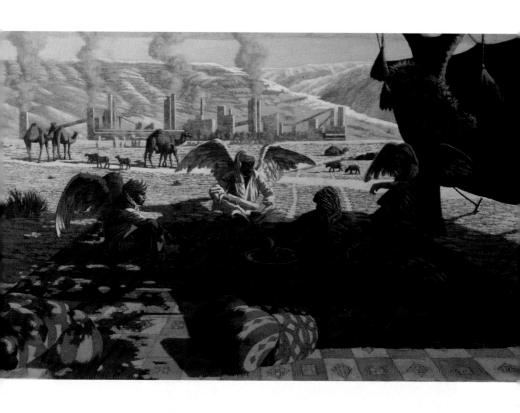

Abraham and the Angels I

In edge-lands of a desert place,
Screened from the white and beating heat,
Are three men in a square of shade
Cross-legged beneath a Bedou tent

Who sit on hot, thick, carpet layers
And wait to drink sweet, grateful tea
While woolly shapes of panting sheep
Lie shadowed by their ruined folds.

Are wings here mirage metaphors
Appearing in this flowing heat,
A mind-conjured intensity
As when two colours touch and meet?

The promise that the strangers make
Provokes a deep embarrassment
Behind the curtains of the tent
Where women in the stuffy heat

Are giggling as they overhear
A prophecy that makes no sense:
That age might bring a child at last
That hope might come when hope is past.

But as the strangers rise to go
And set off through that beating heat
They leave one final prophecy
That seems a promise of defeat.

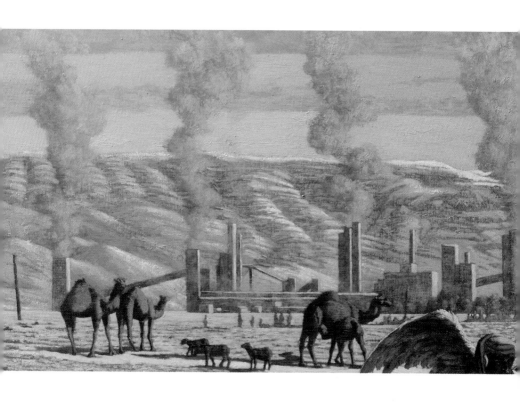

Four plumes of smoke which rise above
Gomorrah's distant factory, are
Four signs of an apocalypse
About to overwhelm the land.

What motive might an angel have
To share a burden of despair,
Unless intending to provoke
The protest which will follow there?

The careful anxious haggling
As with the owner of a well
Is when the story steps outside
That which it had appeared to tell

And offers hospitality
To that which leads beyond despair
And opens up the tented mind
And welcomes angels unaware.

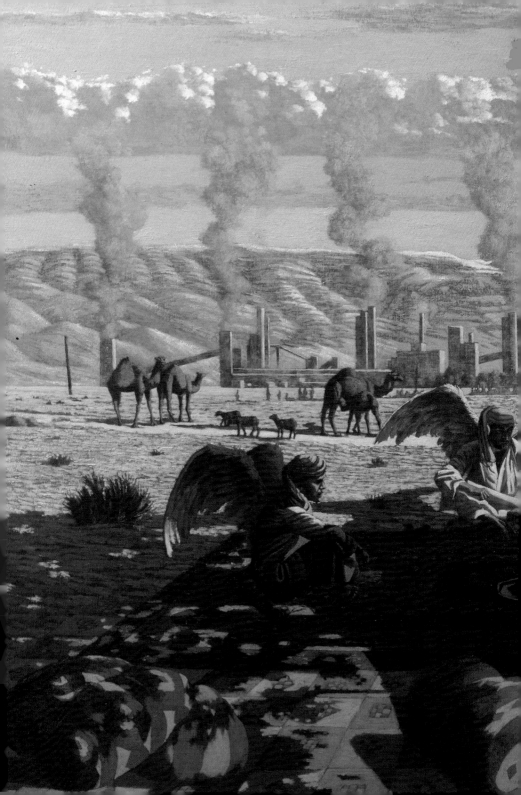

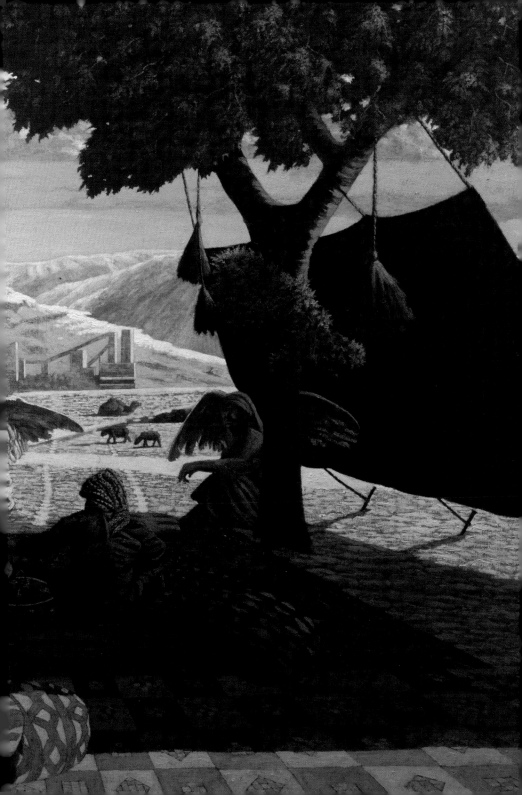

Seven Songs for Isseos

Deir al-Zor, Thursday 10 October 1996

From Deir al-Zor the bus travelled on a road parallel to the Euphrates, scattered with tented Bedouin villages and small flocks of sheep and goats being driven by boys along the road, or crammed into the back of tiny open vans. Whenever the bus passed people would wave from the side of the road. I longed to stop and get out. I felt, as Van Gogh did at Drempter, that I could spend a lifetime painting along this road – but there was no halt until we arrived at Mari.

Somehow the excavations at Mari convey a sense of extraordinary antiquity – the descent into the midst of the massive walls, covered now by a plastic roof, feels like climbing down into the foundations of time. And this really is old: the deepest layer has been dated to 2900 BC – perhaps a thousand years before Abraham passed this way on his journey from Ur.

Retracing our steps along the road, we arrived in the late afternoon outside the walls of a ruined town on the edge of the Euphrates. This was Dura-Europos. Passing through the massive Palmyra gate we found ourselves walking through the streets of a complete Roman city. A vast desolation. It's extraordinary here, as so often in Syria, to find yourself entirely alone in such places. The guard of the site offered to ride us round it on his motorcycle, but instead we walked in the beautiful evening light down to the impressive Jewish synagogue where a great fresco cycle was found when the site was excavated in the 1930s.

From there we walked across to the palace of the Roman governor which commands a glorious view over the Euphrates. It was still baking hot in the sun but I tried (not very successfully) to do a sketch. Looking down from this height surrounded by thick walls and the desert behind you, it's easy to see why this outpost of the Roman imperium might have felt fatally secure from the Sassanian empire across the river.

I was sure that somewhere on this site was a Christian house church. The guide denied it, but looking at a map I managed to locate the place. There was nothing impressive about the building; it seemed to be collecting plastic bags blown in from the desert, but given that we know the city was destroyed in AD 256, this must be the oldest securely dateable church in existence.

I

The *miradores* of the world
Are balconies from which we view
The long horizons of our lives
Transforming to transparent blue.
The many lands become as one,
A thousand views become one whole,
The absolutes of distance touch
Some absolute within the soul.
And while the palace on the heights
Has settled far down into time
Its high perspective still incites
The eye to follow as it shows
The river's slowly winding flows
Towards an endless blue sublime.

The faint sounds of a flock of sheep
Ride on the winds from far below
Up to the heights where Isseos scents
The cooking smoke, and sees it blow
From hearths throughout the army town.
A sentry on the northern wall,
From where the *Dux Ripae* looks down,
He hears the signal trumpet call
And marches out towards the tower
Where Proclus stands to take the roll.
But as the trumpet marks the hour,
A moment in that evening heat
Ignites, as when two empires meet,
Some absolute within his soul.

The river flows through desert lands
And leaves in passing, fields of green
Where crops grow through the arid sands
And wilderness is thick with wheat.
The river flows where empires meet
And all allegiance is aligned;
Where thoughts resolve, and choice is made
Between opposing states of mind.
So Isseos standing on that height,
As in a moment out of time,
Finds in that evening's fading light
Some absolute within his soul
Which draws him like his own heart's goal
Towards an endless blue sublime.

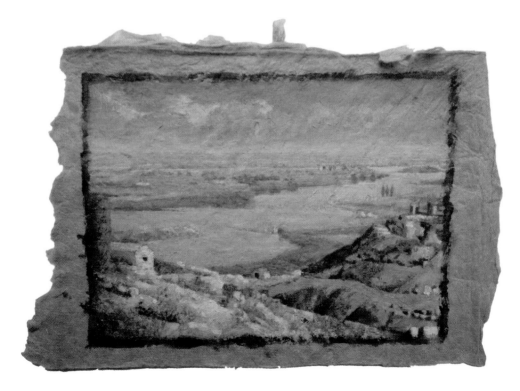

Deir al-Zor, Wednesday 13 October 1999

The small distant dust storms we saw swirling out in the desert yester-day seem to have been forerunners of the real thing. We were standing by the Roman fort in Dura-Europos looking at a flock of goats being watered on the banks of the Euphrates some hundreds of feet below, when we noticed that it was darker and somehow harder to see through the atmosphere. There was already a strong wind and when we turned round the sky over the desert had turned dark yellow. The next moment the storm was upon us.

When we got up this morning, the sky had seemed grey and we had attributed it to a mist from the Euphrates. We had some difficulty getting out of Deir. Our first move was to go the wrong way down a busy market street. The policeman who we thought at first was going to arrest us turned out to be trying to give directions which did in the end enable us to get on the road to Mari and Dura-Europos.

This was the road full of Bedouin villages that I had so hungered to paint three years ago. But because I was driving and needed to concentrate on potholes and stray goats, and because it was so overcast, we decided to wait till the journey back.

We arrived at Dura at the same time as the Finnish couple we met yesterday and went first to the Christian church and the Synagogue, and after that to the Roman fort where the views of the Euphrates seemed strangely occluded. It was at that point that the sandstorm hit.

It was only when I tried to wash this evening that I realised how encrusted I was with sand. At the time, it just seemed rather difficult to see – partly because of the yellow obscurity and partly because the sand got in one's eyes. By the time we had struggled back to the main gate the sandstorm had abated a bit so we went back to pray in the baptistery of the house church which I now knew to be the site of the earliest dateable Christian paintings.

Crunching over the sand made me think about how much still might be found here. On one piece of pottery found in the town was an inscription that said φιλτοσ πρ, 'Philetos the presbyter', with the πρ for presbyter written like a cross. Another inscription found on a jar says ισσεοζ νεοθτοζ, 'Isseos the neophyte'. Isseos is probably a form of Jesse. As Christ was a descendant of Jesse – 'a shoot from the tree of Jesse' – this may have been a baptismal name because neophyte really means 'new planted' or 'new convert' [Michael Peppard has argued in his 2016 book that the jar may have contained the baptismal water that was poured over Isseos in the Dura-Europos baptistery].

II

The rivers that have flowed over my head
The great waves that have drowned my pride and youth
Have dragged fear from my side
Have washed my heart of pride
And brought me, old and dripping, to the truth.

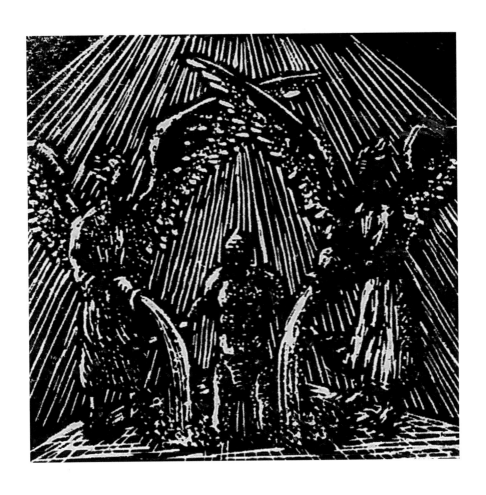

New Haven, Wednesday 14 October 2009

We met the curator in the lobby of the Yale University Art Museum. She had kindly agreed to drive us out to the high security storage facility where the frescoes from the Dura-Europos house church were now being housed (in the 1970s it was found that after nearly 1800 years in the Syrian desert, the frescoes had begun to deteriorate while on show in the moister climate of New Haven).

The outskirts of New Haven were divided into pleasant leafy streets and areas (which looked exactly the same) where students were advised not to go. The enormous storage facility was reminiscent of the final scene of Indiana Jones (I was not, it seemed, the first to make this remark). After passing through security, we were asked to wait in a side room. After a few minutes, the curator reappeared with an assistant pushing a trolley to which the walking on water fresco was firmly strapped, like a patient in restraints.

The colour was much more intense than I had anticipated. I remembered Kyril describing how, when he was in the French army in the 1930s, he had seen the frescoes emerging from the sand and been astonished by their brilliance. The drawing though was quite faded in comparison with the colour photograph of the excavation that we found in the guidebook at Mari (the Bedouin who sold it to us seems to have expected us to haggle, and when we failed to do so was so embarrassed that he refused to let us pay for lunch).

In the photograph, the water that Peter and Jesus are walking on seems to flow seamlessly into the water of the pool of Bethesda in the next drawing. It looks in fact like a river (perhaps the Euphrates?), as though all the rivers of the world were connected. If so, this is strangely similar to one of the Odes of Solomon – a collection of early Christian poems probably written in Syria in the second century AD. There are Coptic and Greek manuscripts, but most scholars seem to think they were originally composed in Syriac or Aramaic. Ode 39 yokes together the Gospel account with the imagery of a river crossing. It seems to invite the reader to write themselves into the narrative, in much the same way I suppose that the Dura fresco would have invited a baptismal candidate like Isseos to step into the biblical story.

I have drawn and painted variations of this scene, and variations on this idea for the last thirty years. All the time I was unaware that it formed any part of traditional Christian iconography or practice. Now I find myself standing next to a fresco of 'walking on water', set perhaps on the Euphrates, that is also the earliest dateable image of Christ.

III

Ode 39 from The Odes of Solomon

Great rivers are the power of the Lord
They sweep away those who despise him
Who are caught in the current
Who are carried away body and soul;
They are swifter than running lightning
Yet those who cross them in faith
Will not be moved
Those who walk on them without fault
Will not perish.

The Lord is a sign for them standing upon
The rivers
He is a sign for all
Who cross the great waters
In the name of the Lord.

Put on the name of the Most High
And you will cross without danger
The rivers will be subject to you
And you will know him.

[I Isseos
Will call on the name of the Lord
And I Isseos
Will put on the name of the Lord]

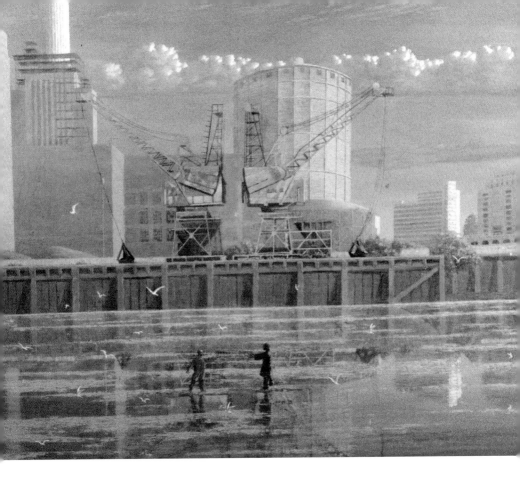

For the Lord has bridged them
With his word
He has walked on the rivers
He has crossed them by foot
And his footsteps stand firm
Upon the waters
[And my footsteps stand firm
Upon the waters
And I Isseos will walk with him and I will not fail
And I walk with him and I am not swept away]
Hallelujah.

New Haven, Wednesday 14 October 2009

The graffiti scratched on the walls of the house church are as intriguing and tantalising as the paintings.

I'd asked if I could see some of them and, along with the 'walking on water' fresco, the curator brought a drawing of an armed Persian horseman that had been scratched in plaster on the wall of the main meeting room. Fascinating though this was, it wasn't quite what I had meant and when she offered to show us some of the other panels we leapt at the chance.

We were led into the main storage area – a great hangar even more similar to Indiana Jones, *except instead of packing cases there were racks that could be pulled out from the wall. On the racks that were pulled out for us were the blocks of plaster that had been taken off the house church walls in the 1930s. On one of these from the other side of the baptistery was a very damaged image of David and Goliath that I'd never seen before. What you can make out of Goliath seems to be wearing armour, like the Persian soldier in the scratched drawing. Above the picture is an inscription 'Jesus Christ [be] with you. Remember Proclus'. Was Proclus a soldier?*

We didn't see any of the written graffiti that had been found. I'd read that these included 'one God in heaven' scratched on a doorpost, one that mentions the name 'Paulus', and another that says 'Christ remember me the humble Siseos'. We did see the procession of women (are they women at the tomb or the virgins carrying their torches awaiting the bridegroom?) where, according to the excavators, the name Ηρας, Hera, was scratched (though this no longer seems to be visible).

There is something rather touching about this literal writing of oneself into the biblical stories, and it makes one wonder about how much this carried over into the liturgies that were enacted here [Michael Peppard quotes a chant from a Manichean psalm-book of around this period that in a literal way inscribes the worshippers into the biblical stories].

The panel from over the baptistery itself, which shows a rather diminutive shepherd carrying an enormous sheep on his shoulders, was very faded. We could just make out a herd of sheep next to him that seemed to be nibbling grass and even drinking from a stream. It reminded me of the boys we saw on the road from Dura, leading their little flocks of sheep to patches of grazing. One we saw on the road to Aleppo, taking his flock over to the fresh grass on the central reservation of the motorway.

IV

From the Dura-Europos psalm-book

We are the sheep of his pasture
And the flock of his hand
And we lack nothing.
We have eaten the bread of heaven
We have drunk the water of life
And we lack nothing.

And I Hera am counted among the virgins
In whose torches oil was found
And lack nothing.
And I the humble Siseos am counted among those
Whose names are remembered in heaven
And lack nothing.
And I Paulus have received grace upon grace
And lack nothing.

We have followed your voice
And crossed over from death to life
We shall not want.
Though chariots of iron thunder on either side
They shall not come near us
Though deadly fumes compass us round
They shall not come nigh our dwelling.
At the centre of all
He makes us lie down
On green grass
We shall not want.

And I Proclus a soldier of Christ
Have been clothed with his armour
And lack nothing.
And I Philetos the presbyter
Have been found faithful
And lack nothing.

And I Isseos the new planted
Have been planted by the streams of living water
And lack nothing.

The Lord will guard his little flock
And no one will snatch us from his hand.
And though everything we have is taken away
We shall not want
And though everything we have is taken away
We lack nothing.

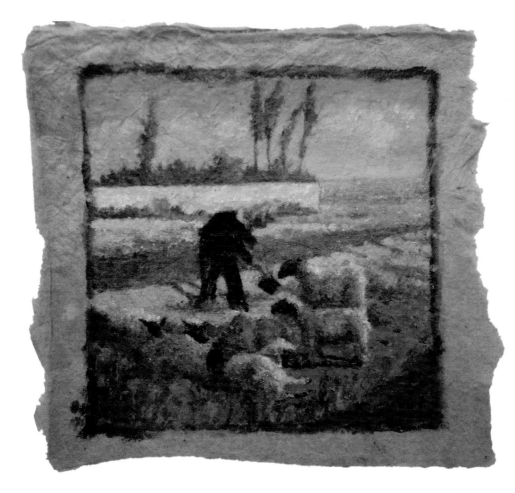

Oxford, April 2017

I have just sent an email to the Yale Museum of Art asking if they can find in their archive the photograph of a lost fresco.

I only discovered the existence of the fresco this morning as I was reading Michael Peppard's book about the Dura-Europos house church. Peppard refers to Hopkins's account of the original excavations in which he describes a panel on the south side of the baptistery, which seemed to show a paradise garden – full of trees and bushes. On the excavation's isomorphic drawing it is marked 'wooded scene (Eden)'. The strange thing is that when the frescoes were moved to Yale this panel never arrived. There is no record of it deteriorating on site, nor of it going to Damascus. What happened to it? The only record apparently is the excavation photograph.

So far no reply from Yale. If the panel does indeed show a paradise garden with a river flowing out of it, it will be the second time I have found in these frescoes an anticipation of imagery I have used myself.

I started drawing walking on water scenes while I was still at the Royal Academy. It seemed to me such a powerful image that I was astonished to find it barely featured in Christian iconography. It was only after that first visit to Dura, when I came across some reproductions of the Dura frescoes, that I understood the hidden well of imagery that I had been drawing on.

I had a similar experience many years later when I came to make a stained glass window (and later a font cover) for St Mary's, Iffley. The window was in what in effect was the baptistery of the church and needed to relate to the thirteenth-century font. It also needed to relate to the Tree of Life in John Piper's nativity window opposite it. In the end, I found myself sketching out an odd poetic image of Christ crucified on a flowering tree from which a river of life flows past a flock of sheep and through a paradise garden, down to the ancient font.

I was worried that the congregation might find this image too far removed from traditional Christian iconography, and took these worries with me on a week's holiday to Rome. One afternoon we walked into the twelfth-century church of San Clemente, just up the road from the Colosseum. Almost the first thing I saw was the great apse mosaic (which may have been copied from the fourth-century church that still exists underneath the present one) showing Christ crucified in the midst of a flowering tree of life from the roots of which a river of life flows down through a paradise garden to a flock of sheep. Now it seems this image too might be even older than I had imagined.

Michael Peppard includes in his book an illumination from the Russano gospels – one of the earliest surviving illuminated manuscripts – that seems to have been produced in Syria between the fourth and seventh centuries AD. The image he reproduces shows the wise virgins holding torches very much like those in the fresco at Dura. Behind them are fruit-covered trees representing the garden of Eden from the roots of which emerge the four rivers of paradise which run under the feet of the virgins.

Peppard points out that later baptisteries and texts use the theme of a new creation – a restoration of paradise and the rivers of paradise. This leads him to suggest that the missing panel was a scene of paradise (Eden) which 'generated a river or rivers that flowed around the room' in flowing lines of wavy water 'underneath the series of mighty deeds'. These would include scenes of the walking on water and the pool of Bethesda, as well as the river above the font from which the sheep are drinking.

Yale have just emailed me the excavation photograph which seems to confirm Peppard's suggestion, in that within the design just below the plants are decorative swirls that look like flowing water.

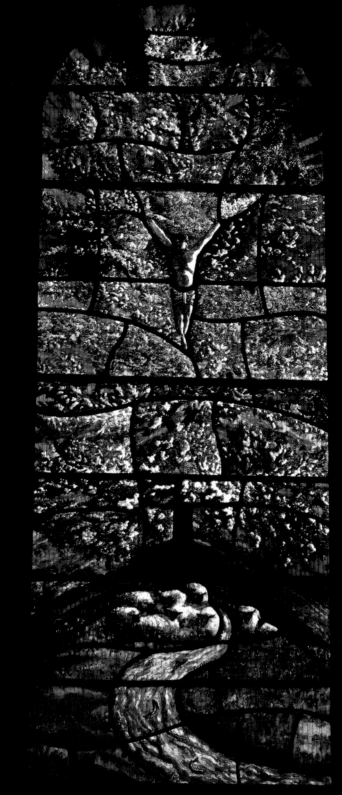

V

A man, a river, and a tree
Enamelled with the flowers of May.
Good Friday sky as blue as sea
A hill as green as Easter day.

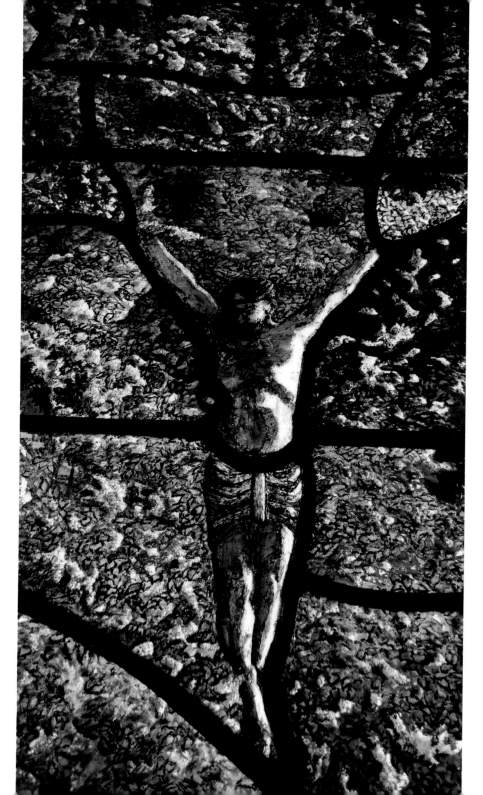

A tree, a river, and a man
Who hangs from branches thick with flowers.
A love that flowed since time began
Is measured here in three long hours.

A man, a tree, a river flows
Down to the font and origin
Where man, tree, river all disclose
The Easter where our lives begin.

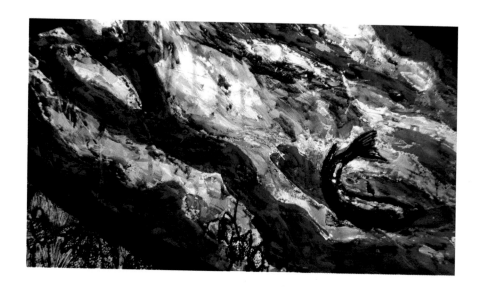

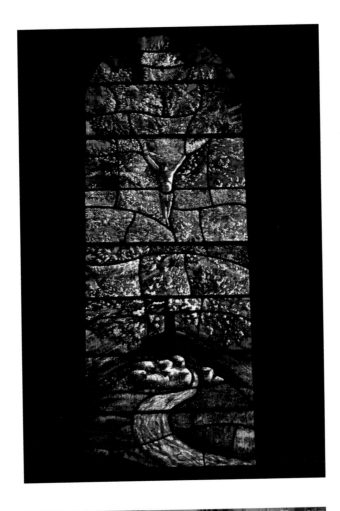

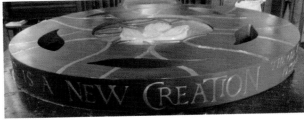

Aleppo, Thursday 14 October 1999

When we set out from Deir this morning I was hoping to fulfil my ambition of painting and taking photographs in the villages along the road. Both of these things turned out to be difficult not because people didn't want to be painted or photographed but because they did. As soon as we stopped the car, people would spring up out of nowhere wanting us to photograph them, their houses, families and sheep. It seemed to be raining pictures. I could have spent a week or a year going up and down that road and not have run out of things to paint.

It was a fine clear day with the Euphrates sparkling away on our right. We passed a great sweep of desert cliffs with a green plain in front of it where people were scything barley in a kind of communal field.

Yesterday, when we got back to Deir after the sandstorm at Dura, we went to the wonderful archaeological museum. We were the only visitors and they were delighted to see us, turning on lights and bringing in cups of tea. We saw a copy of the fresco from Dura that shows Julius Terentius Tribune of the XX Palmyrian cohort sacrificing to the Palmyrene gods. The excellent catalogue they sold us has the statue of the demon god Pazuzu on the cover. The overwhelming impression left by the museum was of the antiquity of this landscape, and now this morning we seemed to be driving past a scene that could have come straight out of the Book of Ruth.

We didn't do any gleaning but when we stopped we were invited to take tea by a schoolteacher called Sl'eeman Abud. His pupils, twenty or so little boys, picked us a bowl of a strange white fruit he called 'Tuats'.

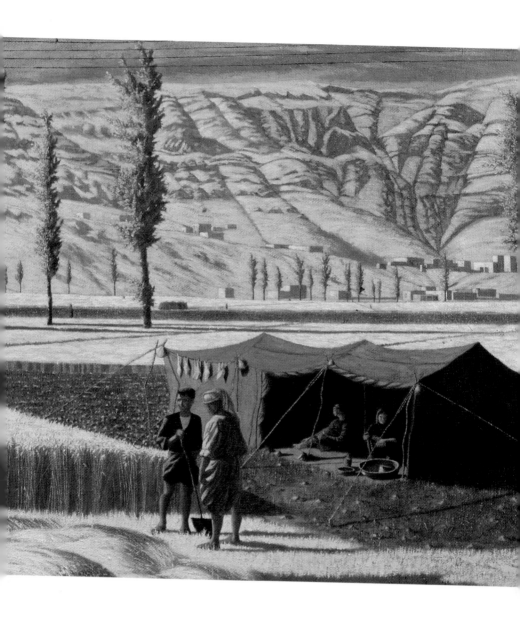

VI

Ruth and Boaz

In this great golden field of the world
Where humankind must labour through the day
And take whatever wages have been earned
With no chance to decide the rates of pay;
The dispossessed, who at the margins glean
Whatever is discarded, waste, and free
Must hunch, and stoop, and try to stay unseen
Beyond the field of what the world can see.
But still an alien in this golden field
Who finding she is seen, and marked, and known,
Whose presence can no longer be concealed
May find an unearned favour has been shown:
A harvest which an alien god will bring,
As Ruth finds refuge, under that god's wing.

As Ruth finds refuge under that god's wing
A story starts in which she finds her role:
An economic migrant who will bring
All nature to its supernatural goal.
The root of Jesse, line of God's messiah
Is founded among sheep, and earth, and turd.
Where labourers in the baking heat perspire
And work throughout the day without a word,
The smile of one who owning only hope
Will find her treasure in another's face –
A harvest, which from all this field has grown,
And reaped as its most unconsidered grace –
Is that in which all human hope is furled
In this great golden field of the world.

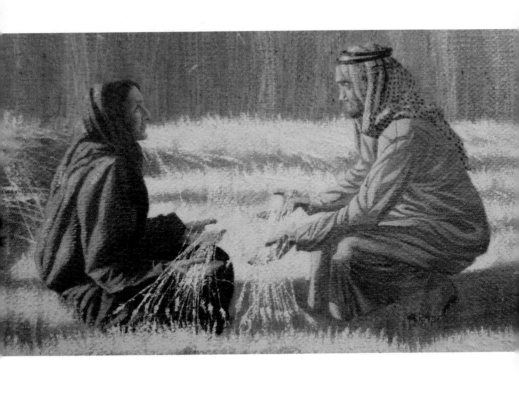

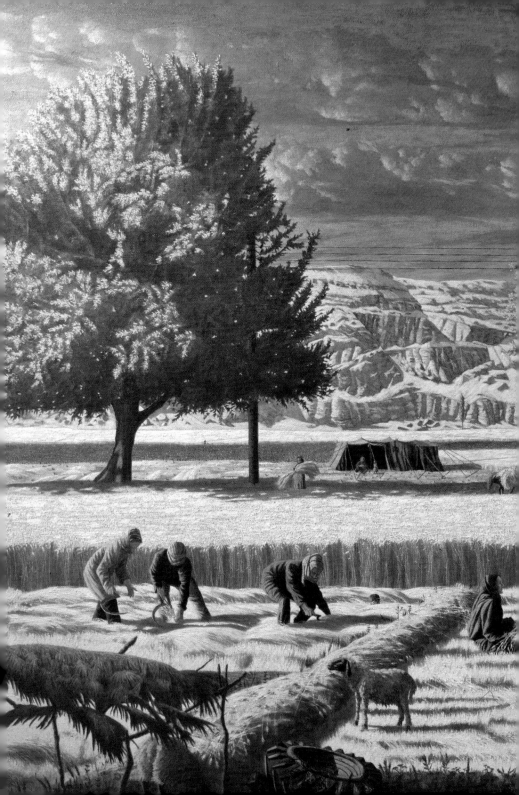

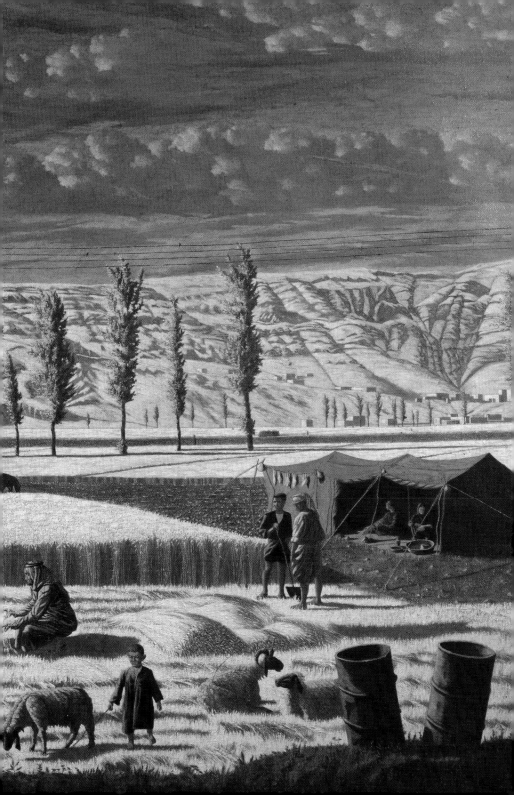

Oxford, Wednesday 5 April 2017

History is repeating itself in real time. There have been accounts for a while of the looting and destruction of the Dura site but today, immediately after reading Simon James's account of the fall of Dura-Europos in AD 256, I heard the news reports of the regime's use of chemical weapons.

According to Simon James, the Romans had prepared for the siege by building a sloped mudbrick 'glacis' in front of the wall and shored up the defences by filling buildings that backed on to the wall, like the church and the synagogue, with sand. The Sassanians responded by tunnelling beneath the walls to undermine them but the Romans, who must have realised what was going on, dug their own counter-mine to attack the Sassanian miners. To counter this countermine the Sassanians lit a fire laced with bitumen and sulphur crystals, which filled the countermine with fumes and poisoned the Roman counter-miners. James calls this 'the earliest known archaeological testimony for deliberate use of agents in the form of gas or vapour to incapacitate or kill enemy personnel: what we today call chemical warfare'.

The first underground attack by the synagogue in fact failed when the Romans sealed the countermine, trapping their own choking soldiers outside. The next attack further down the wall, however, succeeded. At the same time as building a ramp above ground to attack the wall, the Sassanians dug a tunnel into the city. And as the defenders tried to fight them off on the walls, the Persian soldiers emerged out of the ground in the city behind them. Dura was reduced to rubble and its inhabitants presumably killed or enslaved.

In 2015, the fate of the village of Abu Hamam, just across the river from Dura, seems to have been no less brutal. According to a report in the Washington Post, *for three days in August IS jihadists 'shelled, beheaded, crucified and shot hundreds of members of the Shaitat tribe', who had dared to rise up against them. Survivors say that 700 were killed. What has been the fate of Sl'eeman and his school, and of all the smiling people who gave us tea and exchanged their broken English with our few words of halting Arabic? Victims, witnesses, forced participants?*

The siege of Deir has been going on ever since. The Armenian genocide museum has been destroyed. Heavy digging equipment has been brought into Dura to dig up anything saleable. Satellite photographs show innumerable pits over eighty per cent of the site. One of the guards (was it the man with the motorbike?) is reported to have been beheaded. A photograph shows the visitor centre full of rubble and without a door. The reports today are of the use of sarin gas at Idlib.

VII

To sow the fields of time with salt
To scour out memory with hate
To desolate for evermore
The city once left desolate.
To hollow history out with pits
To hollow out ourselves with hate
Becoming here for evermore
A city now left desolate.
Our names are scratchings on a wall
That fade towards an unknown fate
Our lives are lost beyond recall
And having breathed the poisoned air
Are buried under rubble where
The cities now stand desolate.

We saw the Persian armour glint
And through the sandstorm heard their tread
We trusted God and fought our fight
Yet all Christ's little flock are fled.
Goliath played a dirty trick
And Proclus breathed the poisoned air
And when they sprang from their foul pit
Philetos fell into their snare.
Kind Hera carried off in chains
To Ctesisphon thrown in a cart
Wished she herself had known death's pains
Wished she had died upon that wall
Where Isseos was the last to fall
A Persian javelin through his heart.

A door stands open in the sky
The shepherd struck will draw the sheep
And from that blue eternity
White doves will fly out from the east.
The names once scratched upon a wall
Are written in the book of life
And those who passed beyond recall
Are found again in paradise.
As all the flocks are gathered here
A cross becomes a tree of life
And Isseos freed from his last fear
And breathing with the Spirit's breath
And having passed with Christ through death
Is found again in paradise.

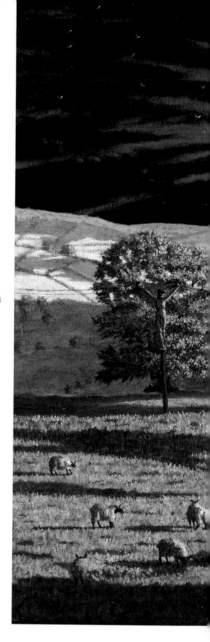

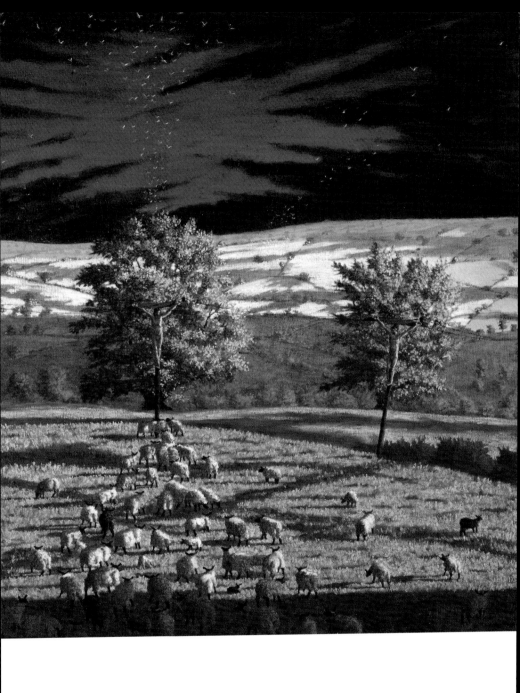

The Bright Day

A sapling in a sea of reeds
Where dark woods form the further shore.
A mountain range of fire-bright cloud
Accumulates to heaven's door.

Some brightness in the soul of things
Still pours through all the crimes of men.
Who failed before and failed once more
Today begin again.

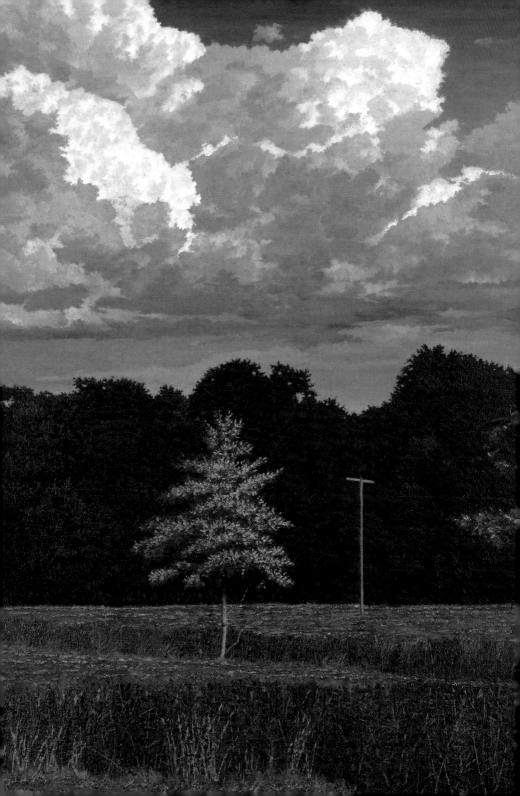

Abraham and the Angels II

While they ate, he stood near them
under a tree ... When the men got up to leave,
they looked down towards Sodom.
Genesis 18.8, 16

A fête champêtre apocalypse
Beneath a day-bright sickle moon
A moment in the flow of time
A picnic on the edge of doom.

A blue and endless afternoon
A grace unchanged since time began
A moment in the flow of time
The angels talking with a man.

White steam from the reactor's core
Our motives burn within our soul
A moment in the flow of time
Destroys the world or makes it whole.

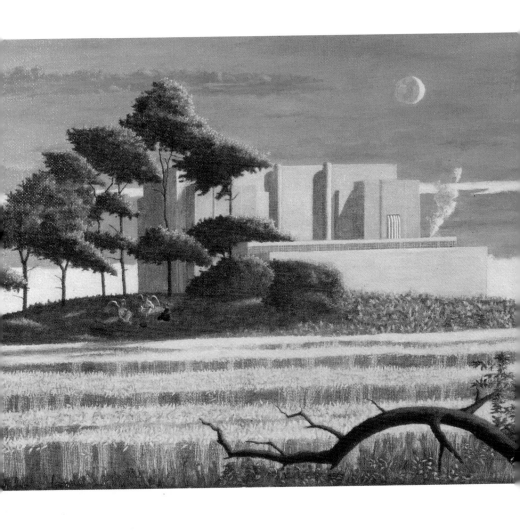

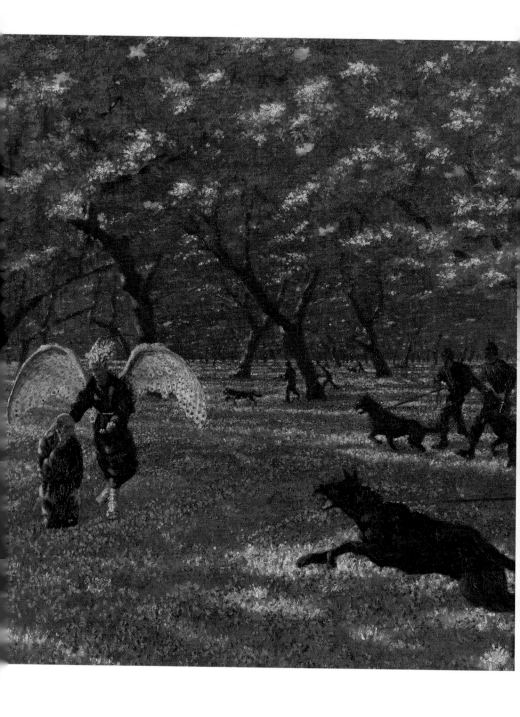

Saint Martin at Andethanna

Not far from a village named Andethanna, where remote woods stretch far and wide with profound solitude, he sat down while his companions went on a little before him. There he became involved in deep thought, alternately accusing and defending the cause of his grief and conduct. Suddenly, an angel stood by him and said, 'Justly, O Martin, do you feel compunction, but you could not otherwise get out of your difficulty. Renew your virtue, resume your courage.'

From The Virtues of Martin by Sulpicius Severus, Chapter Thirteen

Within a river of blue flowers
The images do not cohere.
There is no place in any world
Where this conjunction would appear:
These figures at the picture's edge –
With straining dogs that hunt their prey
While fleeing down perspective lines
Their quarry try to get away –
Should not exist in the same frame
As Martin kneeling on the ground
In Andethanna's darkened wood
In which a gold-winged angel stood
Above him like a burning flame.

Or if a truth does here cohere
It is in his prophetic soul.
These persecuted heretics
Who fleeing from his church's goal
Of forcing all on pain of death
To toe the line and think the same,
Are running down the ages' tracks
As victims of a cognate aim
Where all who think outside the herd
Are rounded up and disappeared.
This desolate conjunction
Is Martin's own compunction
For what the church would teach the world.

At Andethanna, Severus said,
'Where lonely woods stretch far and wide'
Saint Martin told his friends to leave
As in himself he agonised
About a sacramental lie:
The Eucharist that he had shared
With bishops who had left the path
Who neither thought nor even cared
That force always defeats the goal
Of bringing lost lives to the light
Since those who searching for their path
Must in an unforced step of faith
Find unguessed, unsought depths of grace
As liberation of their soul.

Martin of Tours was not the first
To take this stand for liberty.
'The human right and privilege
To choose to worship must be free.
Religion will not be compelled'
So fierce Tertullian had claimed.
Nearby in hot Numidia
Lactanius has said the same:
'All those who set out to defend
Religion using force or threat
Profane the freedom of the will'.
Yet while their stand was just the same
In persecution's bloody game
These lived on its receiving end.

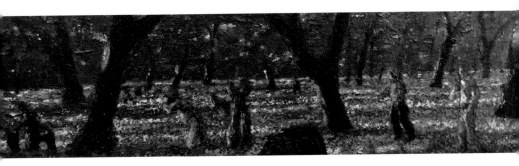

Of those now on the winning side
Saint Martin still was not the first
To stand against the creeping lie
That gospel truth could be reversed;
That love's reverse polarity
Of evil overcome by good
Could be switched back by those in power
Who used force now because they could.
Was Martin though the first who braved
Destruction, to defend the lives
Of those with whom he disagreed?
A thousand years before Voltaire
Saint Martin lifted up in prayer
The heretics that he had saved.

And then that Eucharistic feast
Collaborating with the lie.
An emperor's diktat which decreed
'Be reconciled or more will die'
Had seemed to leave no other choice.
But now in Andethanna's night
The violence of the future runs
Through every exercise of might.
There all the fears that doubts create
Will jump the tracks in human life,
Through jihads, gulags or crusades
They silence every unheard voice
They run through each excluding choice
And through each age accelerate.

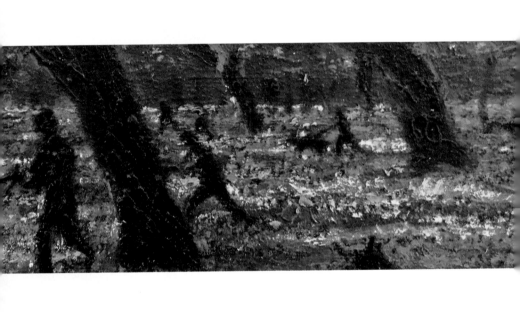

Yet here in Andethanna's wood
An angel is a burning flame
Who at the centre of the world
Extends a hand to heal all shame.
Who knows the crisis of each soul
And speaks to each, with their own voice,
The gospel of the second chance
In which all life becomes a choice.
Here none can watch or stand apart,
When as the thought police pursue
Their various anathemas
Down sharp perspective lines of blue,
Those moments which shape destinies
Like bluebells running through the trees
Are choices running through the heart.

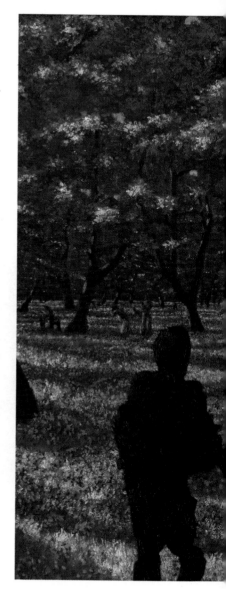

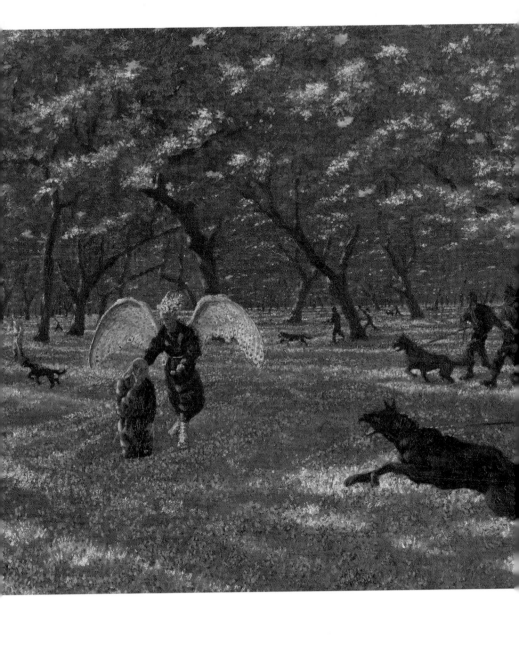

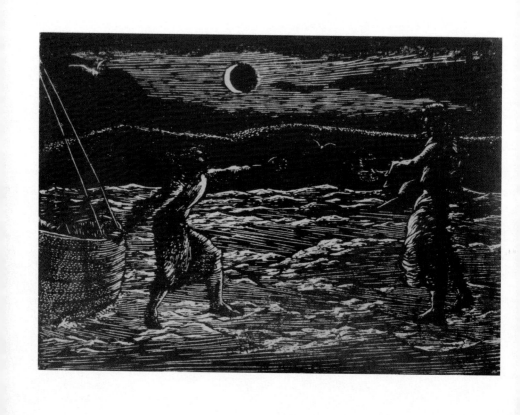

Walking on Water

To dabble on the edge of that great sea
Constrained by fears of all that might be lost
Half-longing to step out and thus be free
Yet wholly unprepared for freedom's cost.
To hear the distant rumour of a love
Which overwhelms all prudent self-concern
Exulting in a freedom like the sun
Which gives and yet demands no like return;
Which rises on our darkness as a dawn
That breathes into the loveless hearts of men
A love which was before the world was born
That we in being loved might love again
That overwhelming love which sets us free
To step out of ourselves onto that sea.

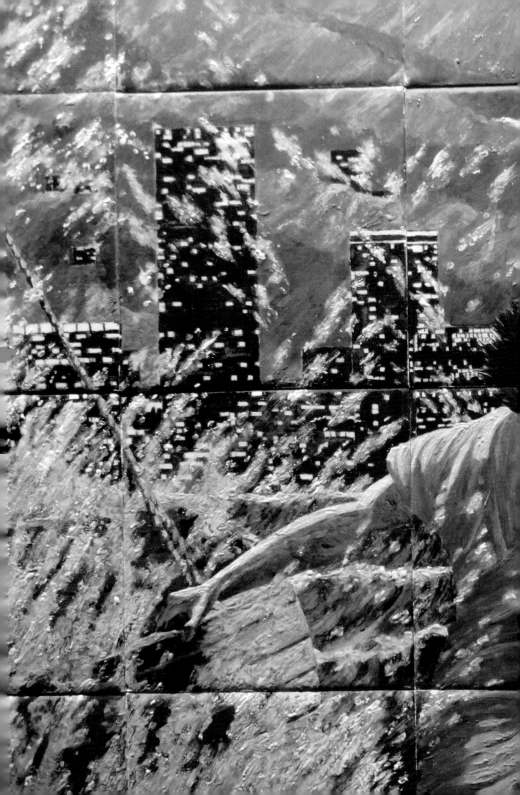

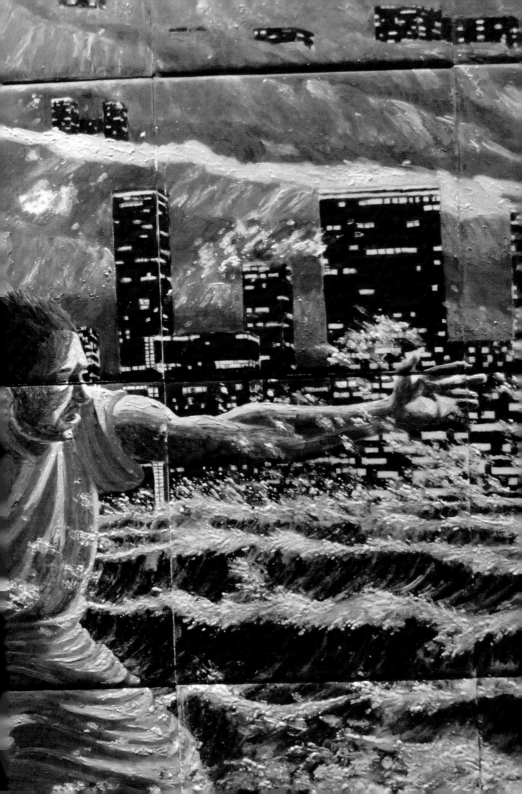

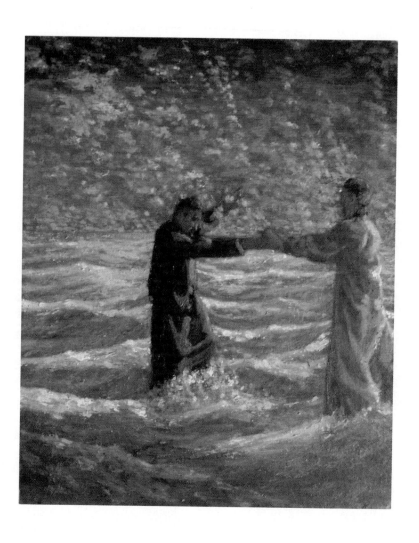

'Lord, if it's you,' Peter replied,
'tell me to come to you on the water.'
'Come,' he said.
Matthew 14.28–29

To step out of ourselves onto that sea
Forsaking all the safeties that we know
Becoming for one moment wholly free
That in that moment endless trust might grow.
To step into a love which calls us out
From all evasions of one central choice
Besieged by winds of fear and waves of doubt
Yet summoned by that everlasting voice.
To walk on water in astonished joy
Towards those outstretched arms which draw us near,
Then caught by winds which threaten to destroy
We sink into the waters of our fear.
Yet underneath all fears and false alarms
Are sinking, held, by everlasting arms.

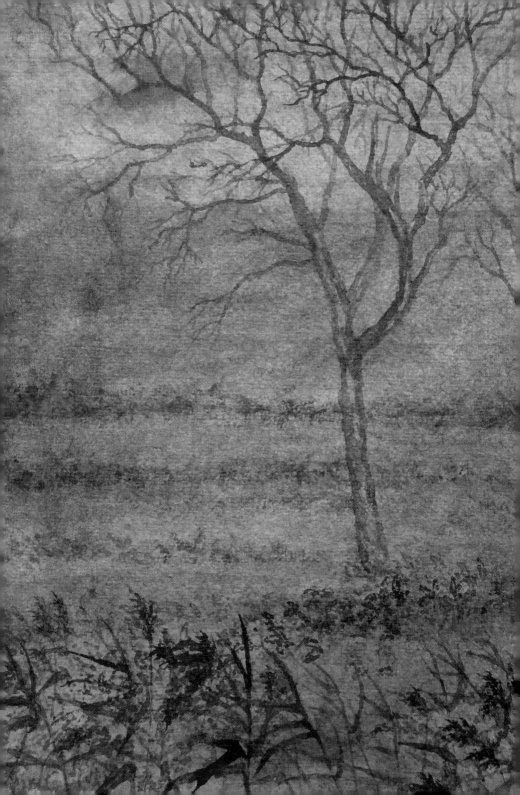

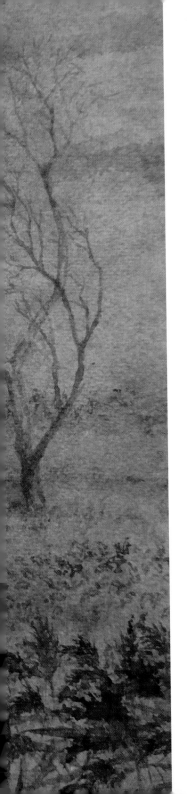

I turned the pages of my life

I turned the pages of my life
And found that there was waiting there
A page filled with such utter grief
It bowed my back
And greyed my hair.

I turned the pages of my life
And found at last a page of gold
A page whose utter grace will stand
When I am withered
And grown old.

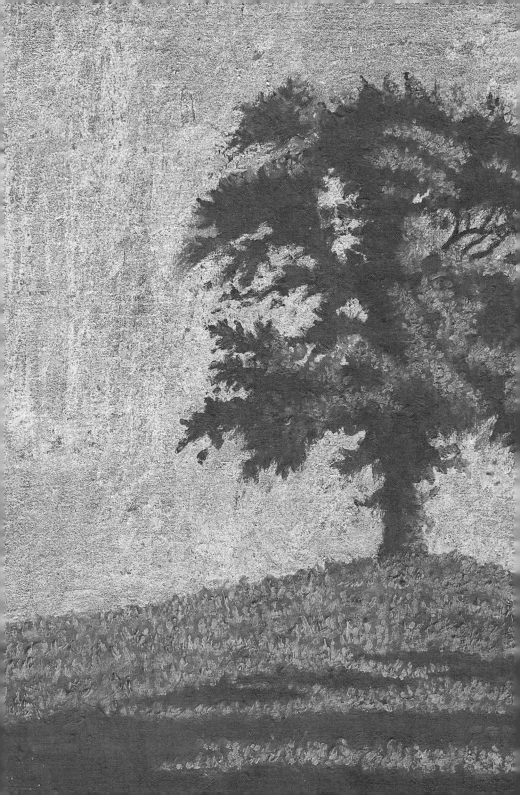

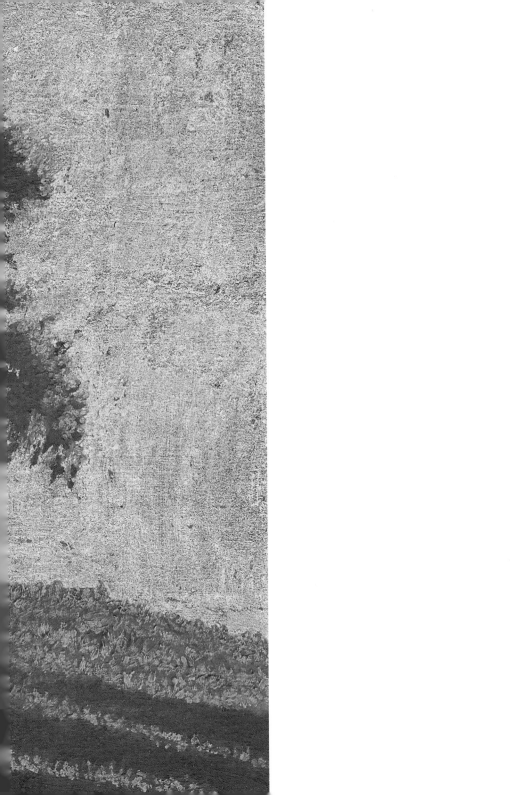

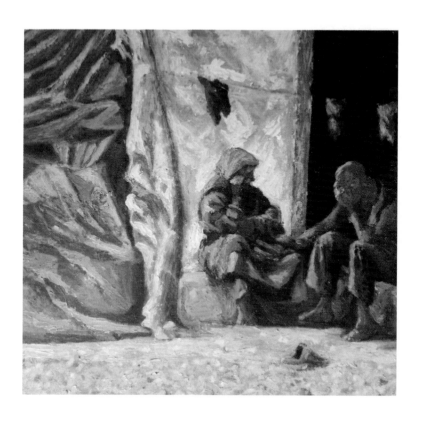

Rest on the Flight into Egypt

Without a home, without a state
Both refugee and destitute
Yet in their arms as tiny freight
And ark of every covenant:
The bundled small and precious weight
Where every hope is incarnate.

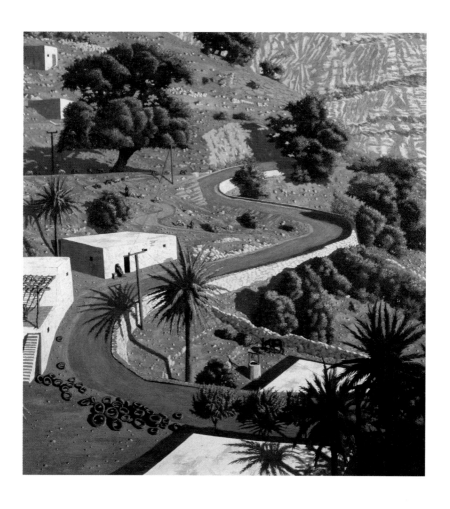

The Road to Emmaus

We found the road *en route* to somewhere else.
That summer's long vacation when we wound
Up searching for a lost site in the hills
It seemed to me as if I had been found.
And when with paint tubes that I'd never used,
Returning on a local bus alone,
And travelling back to find that waiting road
I felt as if I was returning home.
Once faced with that great winding, close at hand,
No lack of skill could blur or blind my sight
As magnetised by that great charged motif
Oblivious of any need to eat
Untroubled by the rising midday heat
I tracked with paint that mesmerising white.

And as I tracked that winding through the day
A man poured petrol on a captured rat
And dropped a match and watched it run in flames
Towards the seat where an old lady sat;
Who poked the charred corpse with a stick and laughed.
Then after school, two boys brought down the sheep
From where they grazed beneath a village tree
And children gathered round so they could see
My painting. And I felt they had the right,
For through that day I'd watched a wonder grow
As colours sang together like a choir
And bound within the freedom of restraint
Became a tune, a counterpoint in paint
A syllogism, formed and made of sight

Where colour patches were the words which built
And shaped themselves into a larger whole
(As sentences may mean more than their parts)
And spoke to something deep within my soul.
So that the trees, the shadows on the ground
The black tyres and the white stones on the hill
Became transfigured by significance:
A speaking which is speaking to me still.
And as I travelled back along that road
My heart was burning with the thing I'd seen
As though I had discovered my life's goal:
A country I could travel far and wide
A world whose wealth would always stand inside
The world which still remained what it has been.

The world which still remained what it has been
Remains, while on the ground beneath the road
A donkey grazes on a scratch of grass,
Released now in the evening from its load.
And on a bench the widow suns herself
Who with her stick had poked the blackened rat
And laughed when, lit and burning, it had run
Towards the sun-drenched bench on which she sat.
Above her shepherd boys bring down the flock.
With calls, and with their sticks, they gently goad
The sheep from underneath the village tree.
And as the sun lights up the distant pass
And self-willed sheep stray off to eat more grass
The clanking of their bells sounds down the road.

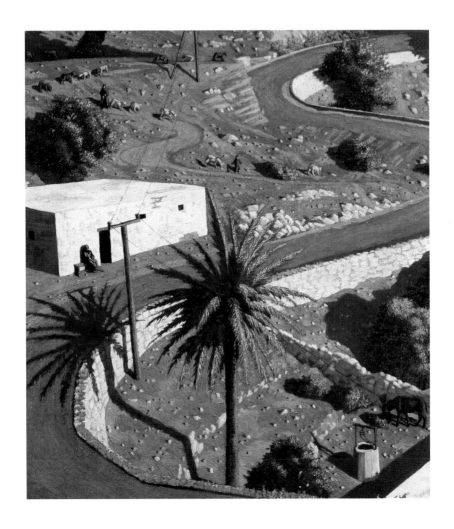

But on a flat roof reached by outside steps
Where three men on a carpet sit and talk
A conversation is about to end
Which started when the third man joined the walk
Through winding passes in the midday heat.
And as he talked, a world where light had died
Began to seem transparent once again
To some strange hope which had been prophesied
In which a broken servant who had died
Would salvage every last soul from their sins.
And as the mealtime conversation ends
And as he breaks bread, sitting on the floor,
The stranger is a stranger now no more
And in that ending everything begins.

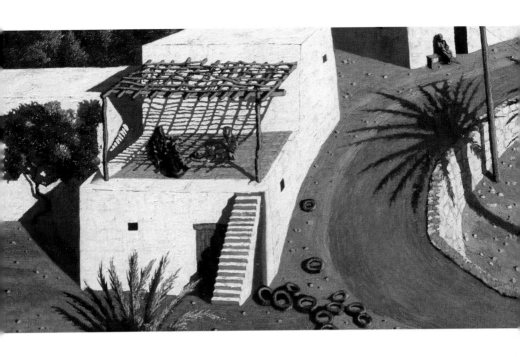

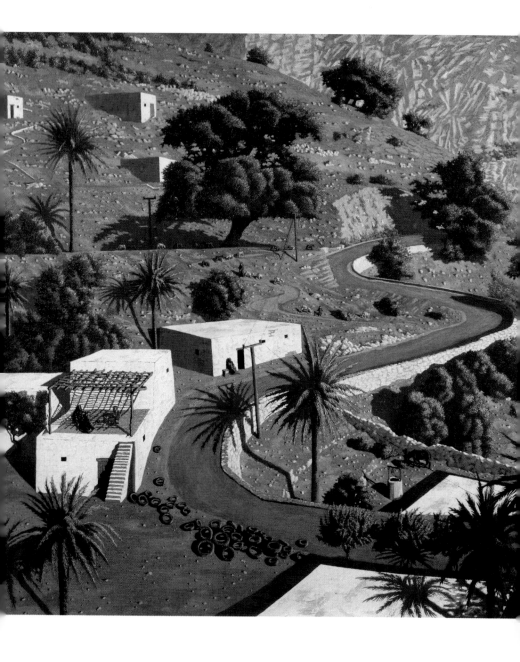

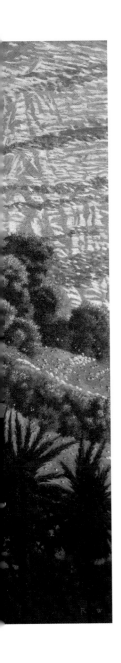

So as the two retrace their steps at night
And travel back along that winding road,
With hearts that burn within them with a fire
That through their lives will lead and stretch and goad
Them onwards through the cities of Judea
And out towards the ends of all the earth,
They stumble drenched with spiritual grace.
As those who through despair have found new birth,
And losing all and giving up their lives
Gain access to incalculable wealth.
Yet wealth whose deepest nature will demand
They traverse all the missing terms of faith
And walk along a winding path of grace
Whose road they find en route to somewhere else.

Acknowledgements

Versions of *I Saw the Seraphim* and *Walking on Water* first appeared in *Fire Sonnets* 1984.

A version of *The Mirrors* first appeared in *In a Strange Land* 1986.

The images in the order they occur (with the relevant poem and page numbers in square brackets):

Medusa's view of the world, 2019
Acrylic over a wood engraving from 1998
20.8 × 14.8 cm
The artist
[Medusa's view of the world, pp. 5, 7]

Writing in the Dust, 2016
Oil on canvas
31.3 × 38.8 cm
Auckland Castle
[Writing in the Dust (The men taken in hypocrisy) pp. 8, 10, 11]

Hougoumont Crucifix, 2016
Oil on board
67 × 52.7 cm
The artist
[Hougoumont Crucifix, pp. 13, 14, 15]

Brightwell Barrow I, 2011
Oil on board
112 × 89 cm
Private collection
[Brightwell Barrow, pp. 16, 17]

Brightwell Barrow II, 2011
Oil on board
112 × 89 cm
Private collection
[Brightwell Barrow, pp. 18, 19]

Brightwell Barrow IV, 2011
Oil on board
112 × 89 cm
The artist
[Brightwell Barrow, pp. 20, 21]

Saltings Tree, 2018
Ink on blue paper
23 × 19.7 cm
The artist
[I turn the pages of my life, pp. 22, 23]

Oak Tree with Gold, 2012
Oil and gold leaf on board
19.4 × 19.4 cm
Private collection
[I turn the pages of my life, pp. 24, 25]

The Harvest is the End of the World and the Reapers are Angels, 1989
Oil on canvas
154.9 × 188 cm
Private collection
[I saw the Seraphim, pp. 27, 29, 30, 31, 32]

By the waters of Babel, 1988
Wood engraving
10 × 14 cm
From *In a Strange Land*, 1986
[The Mirrors, p. 35]

Psalm 75, 2013
Wood engraving
2.8 × 3.7 cm
From *The Book of Praises Book Three*, 2013
[The Mirrors, p. 37]

Abraham and the Angels, 2002
Oil on board
92 × 122 cm
Private collection
[Abraham and the Angels I, pp. 38, 40, 41, 42]

The View from Dura-Europos, 1996
Acrylic on Nepalese paper
11 × 15 cm
The artist
[Seven Songs for Isseos I, p. 47]

Psalm 51, 1994
Wood engraving
3.2 × 3.4 cm
From *The Book of Praises Book One*, 1994
[Seven Songs for Isseos II, p. 51]

Walking on Water III, 2005
Oil on board
76.2 × 101.5 cm
Private collection
[Seven Songs for Isseos III, pp. 54, 55]

Psalm 23, 2018
Acrylic on Nepalese paper
9.7 × 10.2 cm
The artist
[Seven Songs for Isseos IV, p. 59]

The Flowering Tree, 2014
Stained glass
230 × 80.3 cm
St Mary's, Iffley, Oxford
[Seven Songs for Isseos V, pp. 62, 64, 66, 67]

Ruth and Boaz, 2000
Oil on canvas
148 × 194 cm
The artist
On loan to St Mellitus College
[Seven Songs for Isseos VI, pp. 70, 73, 74, 75]

Dartmoor Crucifixion, 2007
Oil on board
40.7 × 51.1 cm
Private collection
[Seven Songs for Isseos VII, pp. 80, 81]

The Bright Day, 2011
Oil on board
112 × 89 cm
Private collection
[The Bright Day, pp. 81, 82]

Abraham and the Angels, 1989
Oil on canvas
40.6 × 50.9 cm
Private collection
[Abraham and the Angels II, p. 85]

Saint Martin at Andethanna, 2017
Oil on board
33 × 47 cm
Private collection
[Saint Martin at Andethanna, pp. 86, 91, 93, 94, 95]

Walking on Water, 1984
Wood engraving
8.1 × 11.1 cm
From *Fire Sonnets*, 1984
[Walking on Water, p. 96]

Walking on Water, 2010
Ceramic tiles
150 × 180 cm
Shing Mun Springs, Hong Kong
[Walking on Water, pp. 98, 99]

Walking on Water, 2015
Oil on board
16.8 × 13.4 cm
Private collection
[Walking on Water, p. 100]

Saltings Tree, 2018
Ink on blue paper
23 × 19.7 cm
The artist
[I turn the pages of my life, pp. 102, 103]

Oak Tree with Gold, 2012
Oil and gold leaf on board
19.4 × 19.4 cm
Private collection
[I turn the pages of my life, pp. 104,105]

Rest on the flight into Egypt, 2017
Oil on board
10 × 10 cm
The artist
[Rest on the flight into Egypt, p. 106]

The Road to Emmaus, 2008
Oil on board
108 × 126 cm
Auckland Castle
[The Road to Emmaus, pp. 108, 111, 113, 114, 115]

With grateful thanks to Lucy McCarraher for providing the first encouragement and to Anthony Thwaite, Chris Miller and Christopher Southgate for close reading and kind advice.